BOA
EDITIONS LTD

BEFORELIGHT

BEFORELIGHT

Matthew Gellman

Foreword by Tina Chang

NEW POETS OF AMERICA SERIES NO. 52
BOA EDITIONS, LTD. * ROCHESTER, NY * 2024

For information about permission to reuse any material from this book, please contact The Permissions Company at www.permissionscompany.com or e-mail permdude@gmail.com.

Publications by BOA Editions, Ltd.—a not-for-profit corporation under section 501 (c) (3) of the United States Internal Revenue Code—are made possible with funds from a variety of sources, including public funds from the Literature Program of the National Endowment for the Arts; the New York State Council on the Arts, a state agency; and the County of Monroe, NY. Private funding sources include the Max and Marian Farash Charitable Foundation; the Mary S. Mulligan Charitable Trust; the Rochester Area Community Foundation; the Ames-Amzalak Memorial Trust in memory of Henry Ames, Semon Amzalak, and Dan Amzalak; the LGBT Fund of Greater Rochester; and contributions from many individuals nationwide. See Colophon on page 101 for special individual acknowledgments.

Cover Design: Sandy Knight
Cover Art: "Enteromorphia compressa, ß prolifera" by Anna Atkins
Interior Design and Composition: Isabella Madeira
BOA Logo: Mirko

BOA Editions books are available electronically through BookShare, an online distributor offering Large-Print, Braille, Multimedia Audio Book, and Dyslexic formats, as well as through e-readers that feature text to speech capabilities.

Cataloging-in-Publication Data is available from the Library of Congress.

State of the Arts
NYSCA

BOA Editions, Ltd.
250 North Goodman Street, Suite 306
Rochester, NY 14607
www.boaeditions.org
A. Poulin, Jr., Founder (1938-1996)

NATIONAL
ENDOWMENT
for the ARTS
arts.gov

CONTENTS

*

*

All I want is boundless love.
Even trees understand me!

—Frank O'Hara, "Meditations in an Emergency"

For my mother

FOREWORD

The first words of Matthew Gellman's magnificent debut collection *Beforelight* include *All, Everywhere,* and *So Much,* a gesture to Gellman's artistic leaning toward abundance in his soulful journey of personhood and selfhood. He fills moments of inner questioning with generosity in the form of light, in the form of seeing, and remembering, in its multi-faceted praise of love and desire. While the reader is invited into the muscular understanding of the concept of *everything,* the hand that guides the voluminous edges and contours of the known world give way to what is unknown, untouchable, and unfathomable.

I am drawn ever further into Matthew Gellman's collection by properties of light. I sense its glimmer and sculptural qualities in mirrors, in fields, in the intimacies of interior and exterior spaces. Often light serves as a marker of time, a radiance that holds the face of a past love; light is a necessary filter for a childhood that is reflected back in a body of water, and light blazes in the form of fire. In "Homecoming," the speaker states, "I wanted to shine./ To make my body burn." Therein begins the journey to understand the body, its nuance, its language, its difficulty and circumstance, and ultimately arrival through illumination. Light then becomes a bright portal to personal freedom in the face of familial expectation and societal authority. In "So Much Light," the speaker observes that lumen is:

"...coming off of the mirror and rivering
through the hush of the bathroom

where I stood in her lipstick, pilfered
jewelry, strange dominion of closed doors."

The central figure in these poems lives in many worlds simultaneously. He inhabits the seemingly impossible realms of childhood, animal, spirit, sensual worlds all at once and within the span of a few short lines. Gellman's poems are filled bountifully with the truest imaginings. They are less invested in factual ruminations of the past and more deeply embedded in a lyrical pilgrimage filled with snow, wheat fields, cedar forests, and constellations of bindweed. It delves heart first into radiance, into intimacies, as the poems detail the aching entanglement of bodies that discover their own boundlessness, a foundry of forgetfulness, and liberation in being released from a past filled with its dazzling wreckage.

The poems are anchored by the pivotal figures of the father, mother, and brother. The father exists on the periphery, someone whose absence governs the collection, as the vacuous space he summons leaves all within the familial circle searching and questioning. The matriarch stays, and though her presence is often equally as silent, she bears the burden of presence and she serves as the centerpiece of quiet stability. The most telling of these relationships is the bond with the speaker's brother who appears consistently throughout the collection and who plays many roles: mirror image, doppelgänger, confidante, and a voice of acceptance. Often, the speaker and his brother are at play where dress up signals more than costume; they rehearse and utter the words that will usher their identities to full bloom. The brother announces what is largely unspoken, making known the longing and truths that define them, seeking to move beyond the confines of gender norms, especially those set in place by tradition. The brother is oftentimes the sole entity who is equally as vulnerable, tuned into the speaker's vital frequencies.

The most fervent of the poems in this collection are, "Brother with Rupture," "Brother, in August, with Hesitation," "Night Logic," "My Family Asks Me to Speak," and of course the title poem, "Beforelight" where a young boy is the central figure in astounding poems of collective and individual pain. I cannot stop living in the world these poems summon, the ones that carry with them the ache of realization, where the universe falls deficient of compassion and where the body pays through grieving. This is where Gellman shines most brightly, his powers fully charged as he moves the reader from wonder to revery, through disappointment and terror, and wisdom. Very few poets are able to do this so deftly and with so few strokes and Gellman has mastered this through his keen observation combined with a tender hand of grace.

How does the mind seek refuge when the world does not provide ample shelter? *Beforelight* explores this path of understanding by walking the tenuous *between* moments: between darkness and light, past and present, presence and absence, desire and destruction, love and loss, all of these parts and counterparts existing side by side, manifesting a boy who becomes a man who arrives, and ultimately survives.

Ether is the final word of this startling collection. Mythically, ether is the upper air of heaven, what I envision to be an expansive and everlasting elsewhere. We can arrive at no other place but here, at the resting place of a pilgrimage that gathered boundlessness and awe.

—Tina Chang

SO MUCH LIGHT

The cracked blue leaf of cemetery
that used to make me falter.

Where else could my mind slow-hum
its hours of practiced evasion?

Childhood's smell of tin-bright cold
and snow-dust coating the pepper of crows

that visit the branches of my walk home
through a present I will never be

unhooked from. I want my lips to split
the lit space between the words *dance* and *don't*.

To know my mother before the mishap
of her early marriage, how she walked

to school each morning of her girlhood,
a rudiment, wringing the ice from her hair,

her head turned down and silent
as a sacrifice to wind. So much light

coming off of the mirror and rivering
through the hush of the bathroom

where I stood in her lipstick, pilfered
jewelry, strange dominion of closed doors.

Some nights talking into the mirror,
waiting for it to talk back.

Mimicking her posture, even now,
each dawn a not-music I climb.

*

Everywhere and at once, a thousand roses—allusive, corrosive.
Think how much you must change. Even more than you dare.

—Sandra Lim, "Poem"

REPLICA

I wear a gray sweater not unlike the one
my father used to wear, his beard beginning
to hang from his face in his student years,
dew pooling on the sleeves. I see him
walking the autumned campus with a cone
of chrysanthemums flaring in his hand,
swaddled in newspaper wrapping, each petal
slanted a little, as memory is. It's easier
to go back this far, past marriages,
mornings of dressing for work
in the dark, his voice slick with caffeine,
mud on the front lawn clinging
to each jaded step I'd rather remember
this sapling: my father, nineteen,
knocking on a woman's green door,
and the way the self emerges in the noon-lit
stillness just before it hears the word *yes*.
In this one life with its boundaries
set by snow, its laws cemented by air,
all we get is a moment to think
that we are permitted more than a moment.
I bought it, this cheap sweater the color
of sleep, a little worn at the shoulders.
It is not beautiful like the past
but like the past I wear it.

LITTLE BROTHER

In the photo of the blue raft I don't remember
you are reaching one arm out, staring

straight at our mother, whose hands
do not yet shake when holding a camera.

This is the past where nobody flinches,
the moment you climb away from our brother

becoming the moment where always
you will climb away from the shadow of his hand.

You do not know that in nine more winters
to please the voices in the attic of my mind

I will throw into the frost-storm
every suit our father owns, will toss

the locked-in pageant of the music box,
relic from before the disaster,

its dancer a flock of electric lines cut,
and you will gather what I've offered to snow.

You don't yet know that while our mother
will sleep, blanketed all season by shock,

past the wrecked spires of topiaries
I will drive you home from school,

waiting in the carpool line, hot breath
of a song I don't know on the back of my neck

and seeing your head in its red hat lowered
as the families around you assemble.

But in this photo it is not yet winter,
in this photo what exists is not the future

but only the gesture toward it
and not the fact of our father's leaving,

only his white shirt rippling over your chest
the second the yellow pail rolls away

as you turn to the balled fist of a wave
and squint, trying to see him.

MOTHER, SLEEVELESS

She walks home from the all girls' Catholic school
under the thumb of March, arms crossed, petals
grazing her shoulders, wind pushing into her mouth.
She knows this street: its power lines weighted
with pigeons. Parked cars. The gutter's rough music.
It's the fastest way, but all month the winter
has taken too long to lie down. She wants to be
alone, but a carful of boys swings around the corner
of Erdrich, banging the windshield and shouting,
tobacco wet between their teeth. She starts
to run from their voices, the gray street
and the car horn's sallow bleating, the empty
shirts on her neighbor's lines making emptier
shadows across their lawns. She does
what she's already learned to do:
she holds down her skirt and runs deeper
into the life I will enter, its same dark colors
and the maples cold, beginning.

BROTHER, AGE SIX

Before the tenuous muslin of marriage
had flickered away, before the piano,

one morning, you and I were becoming
in our mother's favorite shoes. Left alone

in summer, the house emptied, nightshirts
draped to our knees, we went to her closet:

open boxes, the pumps glossy, upright
prizes. You imitated her, sauntering

across the cream-colored carpet
until you fell. Then when I fell over you

we laughed until you pushed me off.
You looked and said, *Do you sometimes*

wanna go someplace else. I said, *Where.*
Then you stood up in your heels and practiced.

HOMECOMING

I wanted to shine. To make
my body burn. To unlock

every glass case where I used
to store all my silences

and watch them pirouette
onto the cedar floor.

A brightness in the kitchen,
a willow holding sunset

in the hoop of its dress—
while my mother set the table,

I heard my father's car
surrender in the driveway.

It took so long for me
to understand why,

each time, she turned away—
shame for having bought

the gown for me, for wishing
I'd been a daughter.

I wore pink tulle. I spun
until I could no longer see

my father, in the doorway,
his head in his hand.

NOT MUSIC

My mother was younger than I am now
when she rode the bus to the Halloween party,
the lights veering red yellow green

on the dance floor where my father,
a stranger then, pulls the styrofoam clown nose
off her face and puts it on his own,

then walks off without her even trying
to chase his sweaty back or his brashness.
Since I was first told this story

I've often wanted to keep her
inside it. Wearing those baggy pants,
a brown drink rocking inside her plastic cup.

I like to think I was perched on the rafters
or a seedling in the barroom plant,
pin-sized pupil watching their meeting

from the fern's nucleus of unfurling.
I see it so clearly I must have been there—
my father turning to look at my mother,

fanning the slow conflagrations
of their lives that will deliver my own,
goading us into the game

of need, projection and scar
that will crack and recover
my twenty-nine years

repeatedly, like a dropped glass marble.
Their voices soft with beer,
two animals staring each other down

under strobe lights, the garble
of music between them, something
withheld: here I learn the template.

That night cannot unexist.
I am proof of it. I am still inside it.
So invisible I must be everywhere.

THE WHEAT FIELD

i.

I came to the wheat field
to look for my sister
but my sister was not there
there was only sunlight
fanning the silence
and getting all over
the things that it owned
and the taste of the sunlight
the taste of a white linen
dress pulled over my head
and each time I turn
to look closer at myself
I turn from myself.

ii.

As a girl my mother
didn't like to dance.
At night, she walked
around those blocks
of row-homes standing
like graves in the soil,
avoiding the gymnasium.
She reached a parking lot
overgrown with grass
where she could lie down,
unflooded by headlights.
Could think. Could look at
the imperfect animal
stillness of every star.

iii.

At the school dance I stood
almost ghost at the edge
of the purple lights.
Then, being driven home,
words were heavy-footed
and the field almost broken
by blizzard. But I still thought
I could point out the few soft crops
still cowering in their stalks,
my face always looking
for something beating inside
what was hardly there.

iv.

I come to the wheat field
to look for my sister
but my sister is not here,
my sister is somewhere
asleep in the sun inside her;
my sister lives only inside.
She will never see this night
will not find me watching
these airplanes disappear.
I don't know where they're going
but I watch them go.

BROTHER WITH RUPTURE

Twin hornets, you and I raced the living room, playing our game of chase
until you tumbled jumping the back of the armchair, your left leg
snapping on the carpet, the ligament swarming with purple, the shin
splitting off from the thigh. The cast was chronic for a season,
jagged rainbows scribbled onto it, affirmations, stick-figure flowers
and the names of the kids in our class at school. The same boys
who would later spit on my cheek and throw me onto the blacktop,
looming, the shadows of hemlocks erasing their steps as they turned
to go. I learned to seek refuge in the tough Pennsylvania field,
yellow weed and spurge, in the bleak apprehensions of crows
as they skimmed the pond, not accusing but not kind. You learned
to recover, dragging your shell of a shin through the den, wringing
your hands, encircled by a tentative light that will always return me
to injury. *Hey*, you call from a leaf pile, healed, October
simmering behind you, *You bury me first and then you let me bury you.*

DOE

She sprang from underbrush
        and stood in front of the sun
                turned red, eyeing

the silver house keys
        and the grocery bag
                I'd dropped when I noticed

my father's shape
        behind the upstairs curtain
                darkening his bedroom,

and I rushed, knowing
        it might be the last time
                I would see him there.

I turned back, saw her
        delicate shadow expanding
                under an alder tree,

light making rivers between
        her calves, the woods
                a city outgrowing the day.

She shivered, shook
        the snow from her back
                then broke into the branches—

a doctor

    shrugging off her coat,

        prescribing me the cold.

SNIPE

His low, madrone-colored drumming
skitters over the knotted tuft of marsh
like a siren skimming the unkempt
songs on the insides of our throats
thirsting for sun. I love watching him
dip his enormously long beak
in the water, all of his camouflage
ruffled, wading in before stuttering
into another swoop toward the mountain.
When it was clear that my father
would not come back, my mother began
making lists: where to throw out
his clothes, where to get the pills,
the places his hands had been.
She substituted food for Virginia Slims
and at night tugged the phone off its hook.
She pulled the fern from its socket
and threw its frenzy of hair on the floor.
Sometimes, on the patio, singing
the songs that made her feel like a girl
again, I would fumble the chorus
and the same notes began riding
the starless heat of our mouths,
and though this didn't call him back,
though we knew it wouldn't, though
we could barely look at each other,
this is how I've used my voice since then:

not to be beautiful, not to contend with
whatever question each season is singing,
not even to try to convince anyone
I am sane and going to be all right,
but more like the snipe veering over
this soggy meadow, calling out to no one,
just using his voice to know that he is here.

*

You remember too much,
my mother said to me recently.

Why hold onto all that? And I said,
Where can I put it down?

—Anne Carson, "The Glass Essay"

LACUNA

If I look for long enough
at the maple wincing
under the woodpecker's scythe,

I am somehow back
in the rippling dark
of August in Pennsylvania.

My mother's pretty features
are shrouded by ampersands
of steam, and my father

is slowly becoming a cipher,
the miles he travels a secret.
Though she loves her guests,

hosts well, serves halibut
baked and smooth
on a plank, in her ribcage

suspicions begin to flutter,
prolific as moths.
We wade through his clutter

the following winter,
filling brown boxes
until they swell.

Beyond the closet
laced with dust, our garden's
torn upholstery.

EPHEMERALS

I loved that afternoon
we plucked honeysuckles

with greasy fingers, tonguing
the nectar, though I was prone

to expressing my joys
too clearly among other boys.

Those weird candelabras
of alien-limb-shaped flowers

fed us their drowsy perfume,
that marrow we sucked sublimating

all sense of self and other.
One by one, he pulled the stems

to draw each glistening bead
from the style, held each tube

so I could taste that yellow,
the summer dilated,

and, without realizing this,
he effaced the grandiose fixtures

I'd assigned to longing:
a moat, an imperious tower,

boy rescues boy, declarations
spelled out in ash. A bee

rocked by our heads in syrupy heat,
smudged by the breeze.

A window in the distance
whined as it fell shut.

And in the absence of language
shuttling between us,

I heard for the first time
love's timid footsteps.

MY FAMILY ASKS ME TO SPEAK

My family asks me to try to deepen my voice,
sitting at the dinner table, my sexuality a tapestry
they are coming close to unthreading. I look
down at my plate, moving fishbones with my fork,
and beneath the mess of food, a print of hunters
in red coats, chasing the foxes. In the forest
outside, animals are starting to yield to geometries
of winter, the grids of their antlers and torsos
hardening, tenderness steeled in the blood.
I am thinking tonight I would like to go out
to the forest and try to join them. I am thinking
most of my life I have wanted to give up to the snow.

PAINTING NOVEMBER

There is still music in the trap
of the mind's pale-gold recalcitrance.
You are ten years old and you cannot make

the house look right in paintings. Distracted,
the light sails to your window
and unloads its cargo of leaves,

and beneath it, your father's crackle of bootsteps
tossing your little brother in air.
You hear his laughter, slipping between

the spiderette-shaped break in the glass,
the salmon color of his forehead
apprehending the muscular clouds,

and you know there will be a conclusion to this
before you can capture it, silks
of the lilies on canvas rumpled, the brush

heavy as a cut antler in your palm.
The greenish swoops of flight
you want to call starlings

seep together. Your brother
completes his passage again, safe
in the hair of your father's arms.

Night will come down, as if forever.

Brown leaves in the street breathing.

How is it that love is not enough, but infinite.

NIGHT LOGIC

The day a boy was discovered
roped to a fence, his body an emblem
of aching, the cyclist who found him there
mistook him for a scarecrow,

so pistol-whipped and transfigured by blood
his Wyoming face, his blonde fingers
still moving, trying to catch
the modicum of breeze.

To be queer is to be questioned
on the way your breathing
displaces light. The way you lilt
or stutter. The way a cigarette learns

to bleed from your hand. I was that boy's age
when a man tried to follow me home
in the clapboard college town
where I went submersible

in the weave of roots beside
a crippled fence. According to gestalt theory
the whole is greater than the sum
of its parts. One light tapped on

on the railroad track
becomes all the lights interrupting
the cold. By this night logic
a boy jumps over a fence

or a boy gets bound to a fence
and there is only an aperture of dead grass
to determine the difference.
The man searches but he cannot find me

and stumbles down the mess
of the alley. I keep my head low
and wait for the morning to steady.
So quiet I hear the whole planet.

A boy is a galaxy shoved underwater.
A moon with a fork in its sternum.
A boy is a star in the stratosphere
blinking like something that could be extinguished.

BROTHER IN E FLAT

Through mist, houses blinked awake.
I couldn't sleep again, so I found

my face in the bathroom mirror
and stood too close. I heard you

downstairs, playing the same concerto
five consecutive times on the piano.

The aluminum tendons of small cars shone
as the moon splintered off in the copse.

You would've been embarrassed
to see me standing for all that time,

naked, wearing the lipstick I'd stolen
from our mother, staring into the trees.

When the window stuttered with light
and blue jays, your fingers left the keys.

My mouth was Coral. Vermillion.
Amethyst. Wanting to be seen.

ECHO LAKE

At sleep-away camp, most nights of the week,

we'd all walk back from the showers together

and talk about the girls across the lake—

loudly, so each boy was heard—while always

a sunburnt, sopping-wet kid would run up

behind me and yank off my towel, waving it

as I chased him into the gold-streaked field.

I was twelve. What I can remember now

are nights in the cabin after "lights out,"

when that same gangly boy would sneak down

and press his forehead against my neck,

nights when I didn't dare move in closer

to tug at his waistband or breathe too loud,

nights when we laid there, more unprotected

than our burr-pricked ankles and felt desire

clanging in our chests, louder than the bell

that split us when we all woke for breakfast.

TRYING TO GROW

Should I have taken more notes
about the pig's legs, pickled on the tray?
About the blonde fingers of the girl
I'd been partnered with, her scalpel
slitting the heart? I walked home
after class and stared at the stipples
in the field, the radish flanks of the horse
lit by a rain I could only describe
as sudden. I'd been ashamed to not
make the cut through that skin,
toughened and grayed by the freezer,
the pig's eyes pressed in a squint
as if even in death she could feel
what was coming. So I let the girl
do it. She held down the throat
with its tiny, barely perceptible hairs,
steadied the slightly puckering body
and told me *It's fine, I've done it before.*
But in a boy's mind, what is absent
enlarges to make up a landscape:
spring, desiccated. Another boy, shirt
on the carpet. Light overtaking
the classroom that morning, spilling
through the acacia in the window,
pouring over the anatomy textbook
and settling in the pig's bright aperture,
all of her insides shining, like anything

severed. We spend life trying to grow
either harder or softer, and mostly
just wanting reprieve; even the horse
seems to know this, watching me
shuffle again down the mud-darkened
road, having looked for long enough
at this animal muffled in the pen
to imagine its body asleep, hauled
onto the slab, still steaming in rain.

BROTHER IN C MINOR

The dog got loose when we came home
and you ran toward the patchwork of park,

calling his name while our father turned
and said *Why does he sound like a girl.*

It was a question asked in the dark
of the garage, next to the power tools,

in a low voice, this man who thought
we were too close to being daughters.

Through purple ryegrass, like an offering,
you carried the rescue back in your arms

and we went inside one after the other
and our father didn't talk again that night.

The next morning, while you practiced piano,
keys plinking, he stood behind me in the foyer.

He looked and then looked hard at me,
the door he could see you through.

SIXTEEN

i.

Sometimes a beetle pricks the acanthus.
Sometimes my mother troubles the garden,

her hands tucked into black gloves
fishing in weeds dotted with rain.

This is before bad loam, before
the fall of unspooled anthomania

when my father will leave for the last time
and she will want, in her nightgown,

to strip all the leaves. While she plants
and re-plants the zinnias, my father

sleeps, close-mouthed on the sofa,
autonomous and remote.

This is before the sold house. Before
the ice floe split apart. The moment

she sees me in the doorway and says
Come here. Help me hold this down.

ii.

Summer bleaches the storefront awnings
my father and I drive past.

The hum of music a weak membrane
between his words and my own.

He teaches me how to manage the brakes
and tweaks the radio dial while saying

It's not like we let dogs get married.
In his mind, he's already in the new marriage,

the leaves on the palm trees teething.
He's finished with Pennsylvania,

with his more deciduous life.
On the radio, a pop song says

something too easy
about family. Family:

a constellation of bindweed
suffering a mountain.

iii.

Home after getting drunk
on a golf course, I tiptoe into the attic

and sleep in the corner not yet filled
by my father's pale Jewish linens.

I wake to a minor optimism:
two girls playing telephone

on the driveway, tin cans
pressed to their ears, the relentless hum

of nothing. Goldenrod
lips the outer fringe of the cul-de-sac.

Midday mounts the top of every tree
like a corona. Reliable morning.

Deepening mass of clouds.
A little wind shifting a branch—

my mind, even then, trained to look
for some kind of disorder.

iv.

The ocean takes another pink breath
to relieve its shell-cluttered mind.

The deeper we get in the slash-pines
my mother's knuckles soften on the wheel.

Her body has grown sharp from enduring
the daily suspicions, accumulated;

her utterances spare, partial, meager flies
in a shoal of nightdust.

How knotted is loss' arithmetic.
What will we have to relinquish.

When will I say I am off
in the way she has always known I am.

How many evenings will I linger
among the tautness of trees at dusk,

hornets attempting to thread their flight
to the heady lilac silence of birds,

flicking dead mosquitos into the pool
and pretending not to watch her

long hand lower the phone from her cheek,
no longer waiting for him to answer.

CONNOR

Through the blinds, we'd hear
your mother's tires crush the gravel driveway,
stuff her clothes back into drawers

and slip out to the river we swam
until it was too dark to mirror us, touch
the only vision then, our legs braided underwater

as the horses dozed, dumb in the field.
At what point will I stop placing you here?
Walking back through the curtailed woods,

we heard wasps apportioning nectar, hovering
somewhere between agreement and war.
I still remember the wasps. Waxy

droning. Burnt semicolons of flight.
They shed a red glaze over my dreaming.
They swarm me in my sleep.

*

We grow.
It hurts at first.

—Sylvia Plath, "Witch Burning"

IN SECOND GRADE OUR MOTHERS HELP US BELIEVE IN FAIRIES

So early the women would stand in their bathrobes,
   the story requiring work to uphold, this belief in magic

not felt by our mothers but aided by them nonetheless,
   pasting glitter on the cardboard walls of the houses,

using a clump of moss as the floor, leaving a chewed-up
   clementine, tulle cinched to pass for a miniature dress.

They always made it seem true, these women who labored
   while we were in school or asleep, wanting to preserve,

somehow, this idea the teacher had gifted their children:
   that there were cloud-lives we all couldn't see, a congress

of blue feet climbing an ether, a trail of wing-blurs
   scampering out as we wiped the sleep from our eyes.

PAUSE

Two boys lie in the meadow
making a story out of light.
The grass where they talk half-asleep
is freckled with mustard seed. This is not
a story of wanting to be a woman,
or wanting to go home; this is a story
of two boys' hair getting longer,
the sun a church in their palms.
One of them talks about childhood,
the sister who wasn't born,
and the sound of his mother's voice
when the birds finally came out.
He puts his head in the other boy's lap.
The summer treats them kindly, two boys
squinting at a spider's reticulations
in the marrow of June.

Outside the classroom, it is winter.
The trees are speaking a leaner language,
and the light is too brittle to resemble
a green river, a passing train, a boy.
The bell rings. I put away my drawing
so the other students will not see it.
I am learning silence this way, winter's rule.

SMOKE

Shame obeys its own ritualism
in this too-bright light of Chinatown
where my father sits

with his chest square, claiming
the darkest meat of the bird.
Mother says if I curl my knuckles inward

I must not be a fag, that if
I push my hands out straight
when checking my nails

I'm the wrong kind of boy.
I thought I could trick each digit,
achieve the posture

and freeze the questioning there
like the russet skin
of the Peking ducks

dangling in the windows,
this test just three days after
the boys pelted me with orange peels

on the playground I wandered,
ill-fitting, solitude
a slate nail in my throat.

A little grubby with duck sauce,
aiming for reversal
of the unhoped-for reveal,

not perfectly studied in how
to perform a masculine front,
my fingers descend.

Behind my parents' flutter
of side-eye, there is smoke,
a flame being tempered,

my mother and father's
adult minds discussing
what they might do about me.

SPECIAL REPORT, AFTER RAIN

What's left is the sound of father's shirt
stiffening on the line. Is the long
professorial praying mantis

puttering the garden, glossed
in moonlight, waiting for dinner
to appear and the TV rages:

men in kevlar, slithering the pocked-up
desert for oil and uranium.
When we were all home, my family

would watch these reports
in our living room most nights,
air strikes, drone strikes, a family

shot dark in a car, the incinerated
minds of caves. What I have left
is the sound of a suitcase

clattering down the stairs.
Is his face lit up as it studied
other faces being overridden

by flame. The thrashing, the factless
thrust, the barrel cocked
by someone else's son—

not the quiet gesturer pausing
       to look up at the bulletless moon.
            I stood barefoot in wet grass

watching this smaller hunter
       devour the aphid, killing to stay
            alive, killing only because it must.

BEFORELIGHT

I am thinking of the sister I wish I had,
red hair spilling over the sedan's back seat
as a boy speeds her through the blue vein
of suburb and out toward the cedar forest.
Her finger hooked in the hole burned into the seat
by someone's boyfriend's ash, her head
tilted back, lulled by the driver's junky radio:
Nothing's gonna hurt you, baby, as long as you're with me.
Even now, after years of trying to see her
striding into dusk, all beforelight, all promise,
her dress a galloping of small yellow wings,
my mind still delivers me only this:

that group of boys killing their engine
and doing to her under the cedars' nimbus
things I will not say in this poem.
Not unlike the boy who held me underwater
in his swimming pool, July, his parents
not home, his whole body locked around me
as he pulled off my trunks, how even now
I can feel a small finger twisting my throat
when I try to tell it, if I were to tell it
completely, if I had a sister to tell.

When I find her along that highway
all her hair will be cut off. She will not speak
all summer and no kite will flutter
in her hands. But in winter, her hair
regrown, she will ask me to drive her
to that forest again, and clutching my arm
in hers, she will look out at the field
that broke her, not trying to say anything,
just rocking back and forth for a little while,
silent as the tundra glittering before us.

BROTHER, IN AUGUST, WITH HESITATION

Wanting to be untethered from the burden
of pollen, the garden drowsy with asters,

we went upstairs, taking turns wetting
and smoothing our hair in the bathroom mirror.

We lined up, the other boys comparing,
deciding which of us had the best nose or skin,

inspecting our teeth with a magnifying glass
we'd trawled from some bin in the basement,

and it was our contest, getting a point
for the deepest voice, a point for being

the tallest, a point for which one of us
we thought we could trust to never tell.

I could not have told you about those nights
years later, in the starling weather,

when myself and one of those boys
would slink the fractured emerald veil

of the pond, wiping the sweat
from my forehead, stilling my voice,

the light in your room extinguished
as we kissed beside an urgency of geese,

wings flaring up, re-enfolding to black.
You and I never could tell each other

that in those stammering attic lights
 we shared the same coveting:

the rough palm, the panting, the real thing,
the blessing of being chosen by a boy.

And you couldn't have told who he was,
at school, quiet in the varicose hallways,

his eyes at lunchtime fixed on the trees
because it was easier, looking at trees.

WATCHING THE HERON WITH MY MOTHER, I REMEMBER APERTURES

All afternoon we wait for something
to happen to the river. Then the heron,

great blue, with miserly neck and legs,
arranges its shadow on a rock,

not dissimilar to a boy in a Greek myth
staring at his black undercarriage of earth,

the centrifuge of its two prongs ready
to skewer the least careful fish.

I'm remembering the better nights now,
watching alfalfa fields popping up

from my used Honda, the family
dissolved, my feminine traits

no longer a mockery, and how
nothing could make us drive back

to that house, the answers
each of its rooms couldn't give, grief

the frigid milk of swans
shaking cages in our minds.

We did not talk about time then,
needles of fireflies re-sewing the night,

silence always a native tongue
we abandon and return to together.

We do not talk about time. We stare
at the river quickened by trout, the heron

searching for some sort of talisman,
for something to make its own.

*

But is there anything human without some fault?
And after all, you see, we do go forward.

C.P. Cavafy, "In a Large Greek Colony, 200 B.C."
(trans. Edmund Keeley)

DIALECTIC WITH SNOW

You thought you would learn the milder weather of being a later twenty.
The moment the dark begins tearing itself the same moment
the birdsong's errata begins. But all night the night-blooming cereus
of desire mounted the trellis of your spine and unfurled
as the salt of another boy's fingers ran inside your mouth.
You studied those fingers, turning them over in the cocained
blight of morning, a bartender's, like cracked birch, a little
trying to live in his stillness a while, and you both needed it,
loitering in the water you'd arrived at together, though
the question remains of where you should go once you need
filling again. Watching the sun stream over the trash-heaps,
colts leashed to carriages, straining in their coats,
you stay in the sticky sheen of the booth at the diner
and slowly begin to draw: boy with eraser moon over his head;
boy in a blizzard begetting more hunger; boy with apertures
yielding more apertures flourishing red and agape.

GRAND ISLAND, NEBRASKA

The pillow was a crook of shoulder I'd burrow
in at night, a cough one flight up the stairs

swelling out the choke of sawdust. Did I tell you
the raccoons were so intent on being perceived

between the walls that I often mistook
their scraping noises for ghosts? Pugnacity.

Fetid odors. I swept their shit from the rafters,
hosed the onions, blistered my big toe

and sidestepped a brown recluse
oiling its legs with steam in the shower,

a thick syrup of June bugs piling up
each morning, the night's refuse,

my thighs bitten red and trying to supplant
your indifference with the stink of labor.

There was a ladder planted dead center
in a field of high, thin grass.

Just a ladder, not attached to anything,
just holding its place in the air.

In the window, on the clear nights,
I saw it reach for the sturdy American stars.

It didn't lead anywhere. Day or night
the ladder didn't lead anywhere.

SOMETHING LIKE GRACE

We spent a good while hunting the right
strip of beach to sink our belongings in sand,
somewhere a little less crowded, with a tide
we could trust and a dock we could let our legs
dangle over. But because Nora was tired
and I was thirsty, because the bus we took
had grumbled in late, we settled on a patch
rough with cigarette butts and a woman
with a bearded dragon perched on her shoulder.
We talked about what it might be like to live
in a place with a kinder summer, more petrichor,
maybe, where smoke wouldn't shroud our faces
and we wouldn't have to work so much. But then
when I opened my mouth to say how I love it here,
why I've stayed, I forgot what I was about to tell her
when I saw those few seagulls a few feet away:
ambitious, staking their claim to the shore, streaked
with the white of what will not be bowed,
taking the scraps of the last afternoon
of the season before they shoot up again,
and watching them dive through the thick quilt
of August, nothing but wind around them,
floating more together than apart from each other,
I knew what I'd been trying to tell my friend:
I do not just want to be like those birds,
their tails fanning out into something like grace,
a slick gang careening ceaselessly into the salt haze

we've all come a long way for; I want to be
the wind gushing over their faces, too,
coursing over every unruffled feather,
not apologizing for any part of its voice.

CLOUDBURST

There are so many questions the rain in a city
will always turn into answers. Will there be flooding
becomes: *Of course*. Why didn't he come back

becomes: *He didn't*. But you remember mornings
mimicking the couples you'd seen in movies.
How his hair looked tied in a bun. How he'd use

words like *proclivity*. You met him at a party upstate
and walked home together, passing a muffled campfire,
shapes painted on the water tower, joints scattered

like the season's first flowers. He looked down,
as boys often do when telling the truth about themselves.
It was like that then. He wiped the grass from his jeans.

Now the city is teeming, and you still haven't gone
anywhere. His umbrella still coiled in the closet;
your bedroom blown cold by the unfinished fact

of winter. This is how it works: the window
gets stuck, it lets in the rain's slowly darkening language
and you spend an afternoon trying too hard to close it.

ROB

Light doesn't have to move forward.
It can confuse itself, reroute after pausing.

The spiderweb between you and the sky
as it is wracked by rain. I spent years inside

the collapsing of the great untenable elms,
the middle C you strummed

become the sound of what had fallen.
You'd play the early morning

and I'd notice something floating
behind you, happiness, maybe, or sunlight

licking the pollen from its fingertips,
and flushed on your mattress, discussing

our families again, the split lakes
of their wreckage, I didn't know what you meant

when you said abandoning a past
can also preserve it. Small kingdom

of takeout boxes, pale music,
the sweat greasing your clavicle,

breaking out your long coat for November—
I didn't think it would finish us.

The light we inscribed in that room
has not abated. Has not ended for me.

I looked out the window until your face
turned silver with the rain.

NEW YEAR'S EVE IN DRESHER, PENNSYLVANIA

Idle in the gas station parking lot, the old grief
cycles through me. I turn the dial on the radio,
cruising each channel, not landing in one place.
Years ago this was a Chinese restaurant

and before that it was a scrap-wood shed,
pools of young cows thickening
the soft edge of the field at night. Junes ago
I was still the boy your hair grew longer for.

In spring, I learned to be still to catch
what wing of you the season could give.
Even now, removed from our city, your grainy
voice takes shape in the passenger seat,

exigent as the trucks that rattle the lampposts
on this side of the highway. I turn the key
in the ignition and will myself to drive to a party—
the holes in the backroads shining, indented

like skins of fruit neglected too long—
and I look up at the stars, which said
so little to me as a child, but whose stillness
instructs me in the persistent gift of burning.

TYLER

He'd get off work at the restaurant and come over late
and adjust his flat-brimmed hat. He'd say, *I'm sorry
I've been the worst.* Then he'd say, *I want to rip you
open.* He'd talk of his hatred for New Jersey, firewood
rotting on the porch, his mother's dumb husband.
When I told him, drunk, I think we're all here to do
something, he said he didn't really know. He was called
maricón at his last job and his friends live scattered
all over, and this year on Mother's Day, when he fought
with his mother, he threw the azaleas he'd bought
on the doormat. Once, he said that his brother
and his friends poured a bucket of ice on his head
in the garden, holding his legs down, his mother
in the kitchen, salting the dinner and not intervening,
and once, Tyler watched from the grass as the boys
poked an injured bird with a stick on the pavement
for half an hour, the bird trying to haul itself back
into wind with one infuriated wing. So it makes sense
that Tyler keeps moving from one red-throated city
to another. It makes sense that Tyler's first boyfriend
only fucked him from behind. And I can see why Tyler
stumbles when he walks, even with wide open space,
and why he only fucks me from behind, at my apartment,
over the boxspring, and late. What we fill with our sadness
we end up tearing a little, sometimes all the way open,
no matter how we want to fix the broken architecture
of wings. For every bird baking on asphalt there's a boy

years later, far from home, filling another boy's bedroom
with the softer parts of himself that Tyler wanted me
to see. Feeling my hands pulled straight back behind me,
my face avoiding its reflection in the window, I think
yes, we are all meant for something, and Tyler left
something out of the story: the part where the creature
accepts it, where its body just stops attempting the air,
where it's wiser to lie down into the pain, to get
comfortable choosing the ground.

MOTHER, AFTER THE HURRICANE

Later in her life, when she fell in love
with the new house, the stillness
surrounding her, she and I walked

the constant field without saying anything.
This was always our way, but the silence
was different now, less open space;

maybe our bodies were closer together,
something bright sewn into the middle.
Amazing how this weather goes on,

she says, looking up, and I nod.
There's hardly a stammer in the sky
and every bird continues beating.

I was the only one who stayed,
she says, jumping over the stream,
the sun in her hair revealing the full red.

HUNT

When the desk spits out the black fist
of a black widow, Father, you hardly blink.
It was you who taught me only small things
should fear small things. In Prague one year,
in spring, we crossed the Liben Bridge
where a conspiracy of spiders spun
their violin-like traps. Panic rode my legs
that morning. Nothing like this has happened since.
Now you take off your shoe to strike
at the hourglass sternum stuck in a corner,
the red spot at the heart of its body
shining like a detonator, elegant stain
against the eggshell walls of your old office.
Part of me wants to capture it, release it
to what wings it will chew on, swallow
the crumbs of regret in my trachea's basement
and show you a merciful son.
But I also want to smash it, snuff it out
with the hands you've given me,
the predatory slink of its limbs
come noiseless, the way most danger does.
When I throw off the bridle of bitterness
time has hitched me to, when I say to myself
We are sorry, we have both tried to be good,
I like to think of you back in this office,
a book rustling on your desk,
the spider still clothed in sleep in the drawer,

and so what if it never happened
like this? I choose to remember
a spider, pausing, looking up at us
in admonishment, and our shadows
taut against the wall, united in this small slaying.

SAINT TIMOTHY'S SCHOOL, 1975

It is natural for us to want to be cradled
says the nun who clutches the fake toy baby
after rapping your open palm with a ruler
for being late to Home Economics.
You scuttle toward the back of the classroom
and cannot help but notice, Mother, the dense
relief of the gray trees riddled with white sun
emptying each of snow. Your mind knows
how to carry you far, alert but sullen
in your household, half-asleep on your feet
as you spread jam and cheese onto bread
for your father, or sulking on your walks home,
asymmetrical whirr of light leaking out of the bars
that same light I passed in my twenties,
upstate New York, summer fully turned on.
The night a green bottle hurtled past my car
and smashed on the pavement in front of me,
I'd just left a gay bar to smoke and watch dragonflies
sputter out in the cracks on the sidewalk.
I froze as the men drove off, murmuring
fag, accelerating into the blackness
as the beer-foam rivered out, collapsing
like the rhetoric of this performative era.
Our loneliness is a lineage heavy as a heatwave,
inevitable as a blizzard, and though
I rarely admit this, Mother, that night
I'd have liked to be scooped by your hands,

hands that tied your hair tight for the journey
so you could endure the whoosh of cold
and the passing cars and the passing jeers
of the boys who rode inside them.
Shaking into myself this morning, I see
the grimness of swans on water,
hovering girls in a rectory, feathers
fastened to an ineffable wind.
I have never prayed at St. Timothy's Cathedral
or stared at his face in edifice,
but according to the scripture
he was a timid, compassionate man.

ALPENGLOW

Riding over the water's enamel
cold leaks from the sap. A fish

slows his heart in the hollows, flecks
of his spine a sequined rind of sun.

I wanted my mouth to split the lit space
between the words *dance* and *don't*,

slipping out of the dress mother bought me
before it was thrown away, not turning

from loneliness, really, just learning
to treat it as wind, to make a meager meal

of what boyhood of lacquer and moody
I clung to. No one can brighten

the sky that's been polluted
by smoke's crooked sentence.

No one can govern the past into gloaming.
But I will not make a life out of pain.

Each animal walks with a cloud
in its throat. Each outline of body a beggar.

The train crawls forward.
Light percolates through the ether.

NOTES

In "Little Brother," the phrase "This is the past where nobody flinches, / the moment…" is inspired by language from Marie Howe's poem "How Many Times."

The ending of "Echo Lake" borrows language from April Bernard's poem "Beagle or Something": "and now it seems the soul has lodged there, shaking, / golden-orange, half-spent but clanging / truer than Beagle music or my forehead pressed / hard on the steering wheel in petition for release."

The song lyrics that the speaker references in "Beforelight" are from the song "Nothing's Gonna Hurt You Baby" by Cigarettes After Sex.

"Something Like Grace" is for Nora Grubb.

The final line of "New Year's Eve in Dresher, Pennsylvania" is inspired by Adrienne Rich's poem "Song": "in the last red light of the year / that knows what it is, that knows it's neither / ice nor mud nor winter light / but wood, with a gift for burning."

ACKNOWLEDGMENTS

My thanks to the editors of the following publications, in which these poems appeared, often in earlier forms:

The Adroit Journal: "Homecoming," "Trying to Grow," "Tyler," "Watching the Heron with my Mother, I Remember Apertures";
B O D Y Poetry: "Pause";
Beloit Poetry Journal: "Sixteen," "Smoke";
Colorado Review: "My Family Asks Me to Speak";
Diode: "New Year's Eve in Dresher, Pennsylvania";
Frontier Poetry: "Night Logic";
Gulf Stream Magazine: "Doe";
Harpur Palate: "Mother, Sleeveless";
H.O.W. Journal: "Brother in E Flat";
Indiana Review: "Brother with Rupture";
LAMBDA Literary's Poetry Spotlight: "Echo Lake";
The Los Angeles Review: "The Wheat Field";
The Missouri Review: "Mother After the Hurricane," "Something Like Grace";
Narrative Magazine: "Replica," "Brother in C Minor," "Grand Island, Nebraska";
Nashville Review: "Little Brother";
New South: "Brother, in August, with Hesitation";
Nimrod International Journal: "Cloudburst";
Ninth Letter: "Snipe";
North American Review: "Dialectic with Snow";
Passages North: "Beforelight";
Thrush Poetry Journal: "So Much Light";
Tinderbox Poetry Journal: "Brother, Age Six";
Tupelo Quarterly: "Special Report, After Rain";
Waxwing: "Rob," "Saint Timothy's School, 1975," "Alpenglow";
West Trade Review's Ecobloomspaces: "Ephemerals," "Connor."

I would be nowhere without the ongoing wisdom, patience, and warmth of my friends. Thank you for making me laugh, for keeping me sane, and for allowing me to see the potential in my writing: Lindsey Benjamin, Lena Bilik, Lelah Childs, Nicola Dall'Asen, Emma De Beus, Claire Foster, Nora Grubb, Kyle Kaplan, Eleanor Lawrence, Alex Levin, Sydney Lea, Cathy Li, Ruth Merwin, Clara Moser, Rebecca Morofsky, Agnes Park, Jasmine Redmond, Marcin Rozkowski, Kim Sauers, Elina Schenker, Talia Steinman, Zac Uslianer, and Brianna Williams. And thank you to the following poets and friends for your astute revision, compassion, and friendship: Andres Cordoba, Isabella DeSendi, Loisa Fenichell, Lisa Hiton, Carly Inghram, Emily Jaeger, Margaret Kaplan, Dan Kraines, Jon Lemay, Catherine Pond, and Hua Xi.

I am so fortunate to have been gently but firmly guided by the hands of brilliant, empathetic teachers. Thank you to April Bernard for being my true teacher and a constant compass. I will always cherish the example you have set for me. Thank you to Mark Bibbins, Peg Boyers, Timothy Donnelly, Bina Gogineni, Alan Gilbert, Dorothea Lasky, Deborah Paredez, Robert Ostrom, and Melora Wolff for your sound advice and generosity. And to Lucie Brock-Broido, in the beyond: thank you for sharing your spirit with me.

This book would not have come into existence without the support, time, and structure offered to me by Brooklyn Poets, the National Endowment for the Arts, the Vermont Studio Center, Gullkistan Center for Creativity, Art Farm, Catwalk Art Residency, the Saltonstall Foundation for the Arts, the Skidmore Summer Writers Institute, and Columbia University's School of the Arts.
To my family, near and far: I love you.

Lastly, thank you to Tina Chang for the ultimate kindness of bringing my book into the world. And thank you to the BOA team—Peter Conners, Kathryn Bratt-Pfotenhauer, Justine Alfano, and Daphne Morrissey—for your care, for your hard work, and for making this moment in my life so beautiful.

ABOUT THE AUTHOR

Matthew Gellman was born in Pennsylvania. His poems have appeared in *Poetry Northwest*, *Narrative*, *The Common*, *Ninth Letter*, *Indiana Review*, *Lambda Literary's Poetry Spotlight*, *The Missouri Review*, *North American Review*, *Waxwing*, and elsewhere. He is also the author of *Night Logic*, selected by Denise Duhamel as the winner of Tupelo Press' 2021 Snowbound Chapbook Prize. Gellman is the recipient of awards and honors from the National Endowment for the Arts, The Saltonstall Foundation for the Arts, Brooklyn Poets, the Adroit Journal's Djanikian Scholars Program, and the New York State Summer Writers Institute. He holds an MFA from Columbia University and currently lives in Brooklyn.

BOA EDITIONS, LTD.
A. POULIN, JR. NEW POETS OF AMERICA SERIES

COLOPHON

BOA Editions, Ltd., a not-for-profit publisher of
poetry and other literary works, fosters readership and
appreciation of contemporary literature. By identifying,
cultivating, and publishing both new and established poets
and selecting authors of unique literary talent, BOA brings
high-quality literature to the public.

Support for this effort comes from the sale of its publications,
grant funding, and private donations.

*

*The publication of this book is made possible, in part,
by the special support of the following individuals:*

Anonymous

Angela Bonazinga & Catherine Lewis

Daniel R. Cawley

David J. Fraher

Margaret B. Heminway

Charles Hertrick & Joan Gerrity

Nora A. Jones

Paul LaFerriere & Dorrie Parini, *in honor of Bill Waddell*

Barbara Lovenheim

Edith Matthai, *in memory of Peter Hursh*

Joe McElveney

Daniel M. Meyers, *in honor of J. Shepard Skiff*

John H. Schultz

William Waddell & Linda Rubel